Recent De Novo Bank Failures:
How Important Is Supervisor Choice?

Gary W. Whalen

Office of the Comptroller of the Currency

Economic Working Paper 2012-1

July 2012

Keywords: De novo, bank failure, supervisor choice.
JEL classifications: G21, G28, C41, C52.

Gary W. Whalen is the Director of the Policy Analysis Division of the Office of the Comptroller of the Currency, 250 E St. SW, Washington, DC 20219. Please address correspondence to the author (phone 202-874-4441; fax 202-874-5394; e-mail gary.whalen@occ.treas.gov).

The views expressed in this paper are those of the author alone and do not necessarily reflect those of the Office of the Comptroller of the Currency or the U.S. Department of the Treasury. The author would like to thank Janet Fix and Lily Chin for their editorial assistance. The author takes responsibility for any errors.

Recent De Novo Bank Failures:
How Important Is Supervisor Choice?

Gary Whalen

July 2012

Abstract: Since 2007, the number of bank failures has soared. A large percentage of the failures involved young banks formed during the mid-1990s amid the wave of new bank charters granted by federal and state banking supervisors. De novo bank supervisory choices could influence their failure risk if charter-related disadvantages exist and are large, or if the ability of banks to choose among multiple supervisors results in more lenient supervision and facilitates greater bank risk-taking.

The sample consists of 1,015 de novo banks opened from the third quarter of 1996 through the first quarter 2003. The study uses a competing risk hazard model to identify the significant determinants of failure or voluntary merger for the sample banks through the end of second quarter of 2010.

More than 7 percent of the sample banks changed their initial primary federal supervisor during the observation period. More than half of these supervisory changes also involved a charter conversion, with shifts away from supervision by the Office of the Comptroller of the Currency (OCC) accounting for most of this activity.

The empirical analysis found no evidence that banks starting with and maintaining a national charter were more likely to fail than state chartered banks. The evidence does show that some, but not all, types of subsequent supervisory changes are associated with a higher probability of de novo failure. The estimates reveal that de novos that swapped an initial national charter for a state one and supervision by either the Federal Reserve or Federal Deposit Insurance Corporation (FDIC), as well as state banks that changed their initial primary federal supervisor but not their charter were significantly more likely to fail.

The measures of supervisory choice have different effects on the probability of de novo merger. De novo banks that initially chose national charters face a significantly higher likelihood of merger, all else being equal. Supervisory change variables never have a significant influence on merger probabilities in any of the versions of the estimated model.

I.   Introduction

Since 2007, the number of bank failures across the United States has surged from just one failure in 2007 to 19 in 2008 and to more than 100 failures in 2009 and again in 2010 (see table 1). As table 1 shows, nearly 30 percent of all commercial bank failures from 2008 to 2010 involved young institutions that were unable to survive for even a decade. The high failure rate of these de novo banks is a concern for local communities and banking supervisors because large numbers of banks received new charters during the past 15 years. In addition, de novo banks represent an important source of competition in their local markets, especially in small business lending, because new banks typically specialize in fulfilling the credit needs of small businesses.

The relatively high failure rate of recent de novo banks compared with more mature ones undoubtedly reflects the interplay of a number of factors. The deep prolonged recession and deflation of the housing bubble represented a more difficult challenge for small, immature financial institutions. Making matters worse, many de novo banks put themselves in potentially precarious positions by actively or passively concentrating their portfolios in higher-risk commercial real estate loans.

It is also possible, however, that the supervisory choices made by these new banks influenced the likelihood of their failure. Generally, banks have the option at any time to select from among a variety of federal and state banking supervisors.[1] Some observers worry that the existence of multiple supervisors constantly competing for constituents could result in excessive leniency facilitating excessive risk taking by both de novo and established banks. Supervisory

---

[1] Since 1863, when Congress created the OCC and the banking system, the OCC has supervised nationally chartered banks. With the July 2011 enactment of the Dodd– Frank Wall Street Reform and Consumer Protect Act of 2010, the OCC also became the supervisor for federal savings associations. Prior to Dodd–Frank, a bank deemed to be weak could be denied a supervisory switch by the "tentative destination supervisor." Now, also as a result of Dodd–Frank, the current supervisor also has the authority to block a charter change if a bank is deemed to be weak.

choice also could influence de novo bank survival because it determines direct and indirect supervisory costs and legal lending limits.

Little hard empirical evidence exists on the relationship between supervisory choice and bank failure, whether by de novo banks or well-established banks. Two sets of circumstances facilitate research on this potentially important topic. Analysis of the supervisory choices made by recent de novo banks reveals that a considerable number felt compelled to alter their initial selection relatively quickly after start-up. The high rate of failure rate among young banks from 2008 to 2010 permits the influence of de novo supervisory decisions on failure to be investigated empirically.

This study's sample consists of 1,015 de novo banks that began operations from the third quarter of 1996 through the first quarter of 2003. A discrete time hazard framework is employed to examine the impact of supervisory choices on de novo bank failure. A competing risk model is estimated where the two non-survival outcomes of interest are failure and voluntary merger into another entity. The data set is an unbalanced panel consisting of quarterly observations for each sample bank until it either ceases to exist or survives and is censored at the end of the second quarter of 2010.

Briefly, more than 7 percent of the sample banks changed their initial primary federal supervisor by the end of the second quarter of 2010. More than half of these supervisory changes also involved a charter conversion, with shifts away from the OCC to either the Federal Reserve or FDIC, and accounted for more than eighty percent of the total number of conversions.[2] The empirical evidence indicates that de novo banks that made and did not revisit an initial decision

---

[2] A charter conversion is a supervisory change where a bank swaps a national charter and supervision by the OCC for a state charter and joint supervision by its selected headquarters state and either the Federal Reserve or the FDIC or vice versa.

to operate with a national charter and to remain under OCC supervision are not more likely to fail than de novo banks in the state bank reference group.

The evidence does show that some, but not all, types of subsequent supervisory changes are associated with a higher probability of de novo failure. Specifically, the results of the estimated competing risk models reveal that de novo banks that exchanged an initial national charter for a state charter and supervision by either the Federal Reserve or the FDIC—as well as state banks that changed their initial primary federal supervisor but not their charter—are significantly more likely to fail. Simpler tabular analysis revealed that none of the state banks that shifted to national charters and OCC supervision after start-up failed.

The estimated equations show that the measures of supervisory choice have different effects on the probability of de novo bank merger. De novo banks initially choosing national charters have, all else being equal, a significantly higher likelihood of being merged. Neither of the supervisory change variables has a significant influence on merger probabilities in any of the versions of the estimated model.

The next section presents relevant background information. Section III examines characteristics of the sample banks. Section IV presents the competing risk model. Section V discusses estimation results. Section VI presents the summary and conclusions.

II.   Factors Influencing Bank Supervisory Choice

Under the dual banking system in the United States, bank management can choose either a national or state charter when they first open and revisit this decision at any point in time thereafter. A bank's choice of charter determines its supervisor(s), and also influences permissible activities, applicable regulations, and supervisory costs.

A bank choosing a national charter is supervised by the OCC. Alternatively, a bank choosing a state charter is jointly supervised by its headquarters state and either the Federal Reserve (as a state member bank) or the FDIC (as a state nonmember bank), which are called primary federal supervisors. The Federal Reserve also supervises the holding company of any affiliated bank.

The supervisory choice of a new or established bank may influence its expected return and risk in a number of ways. One obvious and tangible channel is through direct supervisory costs. All else being equal, national banks pay higher explicit supervisory costs than state banks.[3] The cost disadvantage for smaller national banks increased in the wake of a fee revision by the OCC that incorporated a minimum base amount effective in January 2002.[4]

In recent years, the differences in permissible powers across supervisors have generally diminished. In some states, however, national banks continue to have lower legal lending limits than competitors that are state-chartered, and so small national banks might be at a disadvantage in lending to the commercial borrowers that are often the target customers of de novo institutions. The OCC attempted to address this potential disadvantage with changes in lending limits for small national banks in September 2001.[5] The changes reduced but did not completely eliminate the disadvantage for small national banks in all states.

---

[3] Differences in supervisory costs at national and state banks are detailed in Blair and Kushmeider (2006), p. 6. Recent rough estimates in Whalen (2010) suggest that small national bank supervisory fees are roughly 50 percent higher than those for similarly sized state banks. For anecdotal evidence on supervisory cost differences, see Bierce (2007).

[4] This change established a minimum base amount of $5,000 for the first assessment bracket of the semiannual assessment schedule (total assets from $0 to $2 million).

[5] In September 2001, the OCC initiated a pilot program permitting "eligible" national banks to apply for higher lending limits if they are headquartered in states with higher lending limits for state-chartered banks. In 2004, the program became permanent. "Eligible" national banks may apply for higher authority but do not necessarily gain parity with state banks. In addition, de novo banks cannot apply for expanded lending authority.

In addition, it is possible that the existence of multiple supervisors results in actual or perceived differences in intangible supervisory costs or in the tightness of supervisory constraints. If so, this creates incentives for banks to choose or change their supervisors. While all federal banking agencies employ a similar supervisory approach and strive for consistency, examiners are required to make judgments about various dimensions of bank performance (for example, the adequacy of loan loss reserves, the quality of management, the appropriate examination rating, and the need for and type of enforcement actions) and these assessments inevitably involve some degree of subjectivity. As a result, a bank might expect to receive a different and possibly more favorable assessment from another supervisor. Banks unhappy about a previous action taken by their current supervisor might be more inclined to have this view. Banks might also be encouraged to make a supervisory switch either because they are "pulled" by prospective supervisors competing for new constituents or they are pushed by current supervisors seeking a "quiet life."[6] Changes in a bank's operating environment could also alter the actual or perceived benefits of a given supervisory regime and encourage switching. In particular, pressure stemming from increases in local market competition or less favorable economic conditions could encourage banks to change supervisors in hopes of improving their performance.

II.A. Initial Supervisory Choices by De Novo Banks in Recent Years

Table 2 illustrates the initial supervisory choices made by de novo banks annually since 1993, when de novo activity began to increase in the wake of the 1989-92 recession, through 2009. Row 2 of the table shows the percentage of all de novo banks in each year initially

---

[6] Rosen (2005) discusses the possibility that examiners might prefer to supervise simple, low-risk banks and so ensure a quiet professional life.

choosing national charters. Rows 4 and 6 contain similar figures for new banks that started out as

state member or nonmember banks, respectively. Row 8 shows the sum of the percentages in

rows 4 and 6, which represents the percentage of de novo banks that initially were state-

chartered. The figures in row 2 reveal a sharp shift away from a national charter by new banks

after 2002 that persisted at least through 2008. The magnitude of the shift in supervisory

preferences is revealed by comparing the simple average of the percentage of new banks that

chose national charters each year over the first 10 years of the period with the comparable figure

for 2003–2008. The former figure is 25.7 percent; the latter is only 12.1 percent. Because there is

no evidence that the OCC explicitly tightened its chartering policy in 2003, the most likely

explanation for this shift is the expectation that small national bank costs would be higher and

returns lower after the OCC's assessment schedule revision in 2002.

The percentages in rows 4 and 6 of the table show that the FDIC was the primary federal

supervisor that gained from the shift away from the OCC by de novo banks after 2002. The

fraction of de novos choosing to initially operate as state nonmember banks jumped from about

two-thirds in the first 10 years in the table to roughly 80 percent every year over the 2003–2008

period. The state member percentage did not change appreciably during this same interval.

II.B.   Subsequent Supervisory Changes by De Novo Banks

Because new banks can carefully weigh the pros and cons of each primary supervisor

during their organizational phase, and because this decision is likely to be influenced by the

previous supervisory history of their senior management, it is reasonable to expect that

supervisory changes should be relatively rare soon after start-up.[7] Given this expectation,

---

[7] Anecdotal evidence suggests that the initial supervisor of de novo banks often is the one that senior managers dealt with in their previous positions.

subsequent supervisory changes by the sample banks provide additional insight on actual or

perceived benefits associated with the alternatives in the post-2002 period. The sample consists

of all de novo banks that began operations from the third quarter of 1996 (1996:Q3) through the

first quarter of 2003 (2003:Q1), roughly the point in time when the shift in initial supervisory

preferences becomes evident. These banks were observed quarterly until they ceased to exist or

through the end of the second quarter of 2010, the end date for available operating data when this

analysis was conducted. Given the study's 2010 (2010:Q2) cutoff, the maximum observation

times for the sample banks range from 28 to 55 quarters.[8]

The data in the first columns and first rows of tables 3 and 4 contain information on the

initial supervisory choices of this group of banks. Just under 25 percent of the sample started

operations as national banks (249/1,015 = 24.5 percent), implying that about 75 percent initially

chose state charters (766/1,015 = 75.5 percent). Most of the latter group, 679 of the 766, picked

the FDIC as their first primary federal supervisor. Only 8.6 percent of the sample (87/1,015 = 8.6

percent) wanted to be supervised initially by the Federal Reserve.

The numbers in the last column of the first row of table 3 and last three columns of table

4 reveal how many sample banks changed their primary supervisor by the end of 2010:Q2. The

total number of banks that switched is surprisingly high, given the relatively short time horizon

observed. Of the 249 sample banks that started business with national charters, 32—or almost 13

percent—changed their charter and their primary supervisor. Most of these banks (23/32 = 71.9

---

[8] The actual maximum values of time used in the analysis are two quarters less than the true values reported here to permit the use of lagged values of bank characteristics in the empirical analysis. For example, the first full quarter of operation for a bank chartered in 1996:Q3 would be 1996:Q4. In the analysis, these banks have time set equal to 1 for 1997:Q2 so that at least two lagged quarters (1996:Q4 and 1997:Q1) of data are available to construct independent variables expected to influence its fate in t=1. As a result, the maximum value of time for this cohort of banks is actually 53.

percent) elected to become state chartered FDIC-supervised institutions. The average number of quarters until the supervisory switch for this group of banks was 23.7; the median time was 25.

The data in table 4 show that 43 initially state-chartered de novo banks changed their primary supervisor during the period. This number represents only 5.6 percent (43/766 = 5.6 percent) of all such banks. A formal statistical test reveals that the difference in the percentage of national and state banks changing their primary supervisors is statistically significant.[9] The data on the types of supervisory changes for state banks indicate that most do not involve change in charter. Just seven state banks (0.9 percent of the state bank sample) elected to become national banks. The other 36 switching state banks changed only their primary supervisors, either from the Federal Reserve to the FDIC, or vice versa. In this paper, this sort of change is referred to as a "state-to-state flip." Most of these changes resulted in supervisory shifts away from the FDIC to the Federal Reserve (27/36).

The average time-to-supervisory change for state banks was 14.6 quarters, while the median value was 12. These statistics were not markedly different for the state banks that changed charter along with their primary supervisor and those that did not.[10] A t-test reveals that the difference between the mean time-to-supervisory change for the initial groups of national and state banks is statistically significant.[11]

The number and type of supervisory changes by the de novo banks in the sample suggest that these institutions believe that their choice of supervisor has important performance implications. A comparison of the number and type of post-start-up supervisory shifts that

---

[9] The test statistic is a z-score with a value of 3.82, which is significant at the 1 percent level.

[10] The mean times for these two groups are 12.1 and 15.1 quarters, respectively.

[11] The value of the t-statistic is 3.52, which is significant at the 1 percent level.

involved charter change are consistent with the trend in initial supervisory selections apparent after 2002. Relatively few de novo state banks chose to convert to national charters. Conversely, about 13 percent of the banks that started out as national banks from 1996:Q3 through 2003:Q1 switched to state charters by mid-2010, selecting either the Federal Reserve or the FDIC as their new primary supervisor. The sizeable net shift of young banks away from OCC supervision suggests that they responded to the same forces that influenced the initial supervisory choices of the organizers of new banks during and after 2003. Apparently, new, small banks expected that a national charter and OCC supervision entailed a performance disadvantage.

The post-start-up supervisory changes by state banks that did not involve charter changes (the state-to-state flips) did not precisely mirror the preferences revealed by initial supervisory choices after 2002. Recall that the FDIC was the main beneficiary of the shift in initial supervisory preferences away from the OCC beginning in 2003. Most of the young de novos that switched from national charters after start-up also exhibited a marked preference in favor of the FDIC. Most of the state banks that did state-to-state flips after beginning operations switched from the FDIC to the Federal Reserve. One possible explanation for this difference could be the efforts of holding companies to simplify their supervisory arrangements. Holding companies can minimize the total number of supervisors they must deal with if all of their bank affiliates have the Federal Reserve as their primary supervisor.

II.C. Research on the Relationship Between Supervisory Choice and Bank Performance

Few empirical studies have focused on whether and how supervisory choice influences bank performance. Typically, when empirical work addresses the supervisory choice issue, simple static dummy variables reflecting a bank's current supervisor are included as explanatory variables in the estimated equations explaining some measure of bank performance.

There are a few exceptions. One is Rosen (2005). In this paper, the author investigates both the determinants of supervisory changes by banks and the relationship between supervisory change and subsequent bank performance, including the likelihood of failure. His study uses data from 1977–2003.

He estimates a supervisory switch logit equation where the dependent variable indicates whether the bank has changed its primary federal supervisor in a given year. The most important explanatory variables in the model are return on assets and several alternative measures of bank risk, all measured pre-switch. The estimated coefficient on the return variable is insignificant. He does find that some of the risk measures significantly influence the likelihood of a supervisory switch but the results provide conflicting evidence on the direction of the effect.

Rosen also explores the impact of supervisory change on several different measures of performance derived from Consolidated Report of Condition and Income data. He finds a significant post-switch increase in return for banks that change their primary supervisor and no evidence of a significant change in nonfailure measures of risk.

One interesting and relevant finding in the paper is that his results—both with respect to the determinants of supervisory switches and the impact of supervisory change on performance—vary with the time period over which the equations are estimated. Most of the key significant relationships are evident only for the 1992–2003 period.

He also estimates a failure model using both a three- and five-year horizon that includes a measure of supervisory change as an independent variable. The supervisory change variable is never significant in the failure equations. The lack of significance could reflect the fact that Rosen's analysis was conducted during a period when bank failures were relatively rare.

Another relevant study is Whalen (2010). This study investigates the impact of initial charter choice on the performance of national- and state-chartered de novo banks over the first 10 years of their existence. The sample consists of all new banks beginning operations from 1996:Q3 through 1999:Q1, which is a subset of the sample used for this study. Each bank remains in the sample in each year after start-up until it either disappears or changes its initial charter. Thus, Whalen's 2010 study examines only the relationship between a de novo bank's initial charter and performance and does not explore the impact of any subsequent supervisory change. Univariate statistical tests show that national banks do less business-related lending than state banks. The tests also indicate that their noninterest expenses tend to be higher. On the other hand, national banks report more noninterest income and pay less for their funding. As a result, national and state bank profitability does not differ significantly in simple statistical tests.

Regression analysis, however, shows that the profitability impact of a national charter varies with the type of local markets that de novo banks entered. When profitability regressions are estimated using the entire sample, a national charter has virtually no effect on pretax profitability relative to state banks. When the sample is limited to banks in markets entered by both charter types, national bank profitability is significantly lower than state banks, implying a performance disadvantage. The national charter coefficient is positive when the regression is estimated using banks in local markets entered by only a single charter type. This sort of pattern suggests that de novo national banks can reduce any charter-related disadvantage by entering different, more hospitable local markets than their state bank peers.

III. The Sample Data

III.A. The Basic Structure of the Sample

The sample consists of 1,015 de novo banks that began operations from 1996:Q3 through 2003:Q1. The starting point for de novo inclusion in the sample was chosen so that three lagged annual values of local market structure variables could be created for inclusion as controls in the estimated equations. These variables are constructed from Summary of Deposit data that has been consistently revised by the FDIC back to June 1994. The 2003:Q1 end point was selected because it allowed the last cohort of de novo banks to be followed for seven years after start-up, a period deemed to be the minimal definition of maturity. This quarter also roughly coincided with the pronounced shift in initial supervisory preferences away from the OCC, as discussed earlier.

The sample data in tables 3 and 4 show that roughly a quarter of the sample (249/1,015) initially chose national charters and the OCC as their supervisor. The remaining 766 banks started out with state charters, and roughly 90 percent of these banks initially were supervised by the FDIC (679/766). A small number of de novo banks that began operations during this time period were dropped from the sample because they did not appear to be true typical full-service de novo banks.[12]

Most of the analysis in this study is based on estimated discrete time hazard models, so the sample data set is an unbalanced panel. Each sample bank is observed quarterly starting with the third full quarter after start-up, until it either ceases to exist or, for survivors, the limit of

---

[12] For example, special-purpose banks and industrial loan companies were excluded. Several de novos that disappeared through voluntary liquidation also were dropped, as were two de novo commercial banks that converted to thrift institutions.

available data is reached at the end of second quarter of 2010.[13] Most of the explanatory variables used in the models are constructed from lagged quarterly measures of bank-specific characteristics derived from call reports. So each sample bank contributes a varying number of quarterly data records that consist of an indicator variable that shows whether and how the bank disappears and a set of potential explanatory variables expected to influence its fate at each point in time over its life. The complete data set includes a total of 31,899 quarterly observations on the 1,015 de novo banks in the sample.

The focus of this paper is the impact of both the initial supervisory choice and any subsequent supervisory changes on the risk of de novo bank failure. Banks can and do, however, disappear through voluntary merger as well as failure. In fact, the data in row 3 of tables 3 and 4 show that for both national- and state-chartered de novo banks, voluntary merger is a much more common fate than failure. The relevant figures in these tables reveal that fewer than 60 of the 1,015 de novos in the sample failed over the observation period, while more than 350 new banks were merged out of existence. Voluntary merger fits the definition of a competing risk because it prevents the observation of the event of interest, which is de novo bank failure. As a result, both the simple and more sophisticated statistical analysis will investigate the effects of supervisory choice on the likelihood of both types of de novo bank exit. The effects of some types of supervisory changes on the likelihoods of failure and merger are not examined in this study. For example, the analysis investigates only the impact of a change away from OCC supervision to either one of the other primary federal supervisors rather than two separate destination-specific effects. A similar approach is taken for state banks changing their primary supervisors but not their charters. There are two reasons for this simplification. One is the expectation that charter

---

[13] The reason for the start quarter is that in the first recorded time period at least two lagged quarterly values of the bank characteristic variables would be available.

changes are likely to have more important effects on performance than supervisor-only changes. The other is that the number of de novo failures in the sample is relatively small and so it is not possible to obtain reliable estimates of the influence of finer measures of supervisory change on the likelihood of this outcome.

III.B. A First Look at the Relationship Between Supervisory Choice and the Ultimate Fates of De Novo Banks

The initial supervisory selections and subsequent changes of the de novo banks in the sample revealed in tables 3 and 4 were discussed in section II. The remaining data in these tables reveal how de novo supervisory choices are related to the frequency of failure and merger.

The number in the first column of the second row in table 3 reveals that 13, or 5.2 percent, of the 249 banks that initially selected a national charter failed by June 30, 2010. The comparable figures in table 4 result in a slightly higher failure rate of 6 percent (46 out of 766) for the de novo state bank group. The failure rates of national and state banks that did not change their initial supervisors show the same general pattern. The failure rate for the national bank group was 3.7 percent (8/217) versus 5.8 percent for the de novo state bank group (42/723) that did not change supervisors. Despite the bigger discrepancy in the proportion of failures at the two no-supervisory change groups, the difference in the percentages is not statistically significant.[14]

The failure numbers in the tables for banks that made supervisory changes during the observation period show that the shifts typically are associated with a higher risk of failure by de novo banks. For example, five of the 32 banks that changed their initial supervisor from the OCC to a state charter and their primary supervisor to either the Federal Reserve or the FDIC

---

[14] The relevant z score value is 1.22.

ultimately failed. These figures imply a failure rate of 15.6 percent—nearly five times higher than the rate for national banks that did not change supervisors. The difference in these percentages is statistically significant.[15]

If one compares the failure rates of supervisor-switching banks that began with state charters with those not making changes based on the data in table 4, a similar pattern emerges. Four of the switching banks, representing 9.3 percent of state banks that changed supervisors, ultimately failed. The comparable percentage for state-chartered banks that did not make supervisory adjustments was 5.8 percent (42/723). The difference in the failure proportions across the two groups of state banks is not significant.

Splitting the state banks into two groups based on whether the supervisory changes also involved charter conversions reveals that the failure rates were markedly different for these classes of institutions. The data in table 4 show that all four of the failing state banks changing their supervisor did state-to-state flips. This implies an 11.1 percent failure rate (4/36) for the banks in this group, roughly twice the percentage for state banks not making supervisory changes. Conversely, none of the seven state banks that switched to OCC supervision and a national charter ultimately failed. The lower failure rate for this sort of supervisory change relative to the nonswitching reference group is a lone exception to the relationship evident for the other supervisory change categories examined.[16]

The data in the third row of tables 3 and 4 reveal that an exit through voluntary merger is much more likely for the sample de novo banks than failure. This is especially true for the

---

[15] The z statistic is 2.83, which is significant at the 1 percent level.

[16] If the failure rates are calculated based on type of charter at time of failure, including the supervisory switchers, the failure rate for the national bank group is 3.6 percent and the corresponding figure for state banks is 6.4 percent. The associate z statistic is 1.62, which means that the difference in failure rates is not quite significant.

sample banks initially choosing national charters. Roughly 41 percent of this group (101/249) were merged out of existence by the end of the observation period. The rate was slightly higher at 43 percent (94/217) for national banks that did not make subsequent supervisory changes. The comparable figures for both all state banks, and state banks that did not switch supervisors, are both about 33 percent (255/766 and 237/723, respectively). Formal statistical tests indicate that the differences in the voluntary merger percentages are statistically significant when the relevant groups of national and state banks are compared with one another.[17]

A different pattern is evident when the merger rates of national and state banks changing their initial supervisors are examined. Only about 22 percent (7/32) of the national banks that switched to state charters ended up merging, while nearly 42 percent (18/43) of state banks that changed their initial supervisors ultimately disappeared through merger. The difference in these percentages is marginally significant.[18] The relatively higher merger rate for state banks is evident for both those that switched their supervisor to the OCC (4/7 = 57.1 percent) and those that did a state-to-state flip (14/36 = 38.9 percent).

When the effects of both failures and mergers are combined, a smaller fraction of the national bank portion of the initial sample survived over the observation period. Just 54 percent (135/249) of all de novo banks that started with a national charter continued to exist at the end of the second quarter of 2010. Looking only at national banks that did not change their initial supervisor, the percentage was roughly 1 percentage point lower (115/217). The comparable figures for state banks are both around 61 percent (465/766 and 444/723, respectively). Statistical tests reveal that the differences in percentages at state versus national banks are

---

[17] The z value is 2.09 when all national and state banks are compared. It is 2.85 when national and state nonchange groups are compared.

[18] The z statistic is 1.82.

significant. The preceding analysis shows that the disparity is largely attributable to higher merger activity by de novo national banks.

The overall survival rate for the de novo banks that switched from their initial OCC supervisory choice was 62.5 percent, above the percentage for national banks that didn't make subsequent supervisory changes. The higher survival rate appears to be related to a lower probability of merger for this group of banks. Conversely, the survival rate of banks that began with state charters and changed their initial supervisor was lower, at about 49 percent. Greater merger activity by this group of banks is the primary cause. The difference in the survival percentages for the two classes of supervisor-switching banks is not statistically different, however, given the relatively small number of banks in each group.

The figures in tables 3 and 4 include four sample banks that changed their primary supervisor twice over the observation period. Two of these initially had national charters. Both of these banks first switched to a state charter, and later did a state-to-state flip. One of these banks ultimately failed and the other disappeared through merger. The other two of the four double-switchers kept their initial state charters and changed only their primary federal supervisors twice. One of this pair survived and the other merged out of existence.

IV.   The Competing Risk Model

The primary focus of this paper is the relationship between a de novo bank's initial primary federal supervisory choice and any subsequent supervisory change on the bank's risk of failure. The data on the ultimate fates of the sample banks clearly show that merger represents an important competing risk for de novo banks and should be addressed in any model of de novo failure. This is done in this study by assuming that failure and merger are the competing risks for de novo banks in a multinomial logit hazard model.

This model has the following general form:

$$P(Y_{it} = j) = e^{\beta X}/(1 + \Sigma e^{\beta X}) \text{, for j=1,2}$$

$$P(Y_{it} = j) = 1/(1 + \Sigma e^{\beta X}) \text{, for j=0}$$

where $P(Y_{it} = j)$ represents the probability that de novo bank i experiences outcome j in quarter t. Outcome j=0 is the reference outcome and indicates that the bank continues to exist. Outcome j=1 represents exit in quarter t through voluntary merger and outcome j=2 indicates failure in quarter t. X represents the vector of explanatory variables presumed to influence the likelihood that a de novo bank disappears through failure or merger and β represents the coefficients to be estimated. All of the X variables are presumed to influence the outcomes with some time lag. To minimize the likelihood of statistical problems related to unobserved heterogeneity or bank-specific correlation of observations, robust standard errors are estimated for the independent variables assuming clustering at the bank level.

Because the main concern in the paper is how supervisory choices influence the likelihood of de novo bank failure, the first step in the modeling strategy was to arrive at a relatively parsimonious specification for a failure equation that did not include a measure of supervisory choice. This effort was informed by previous empirical work and preliminary statistical results obtained using the sample data. The final specification was culled from a much larger set of candidate explanatory variables. In the multinomial logit model, the set of independent variables is constrained to be the same in each outcome equation and so the selected specification for the failure equation determined that of the merger equation as well.

The chosen set of explanatory variables included eight measures of each bank's financial condition or organization. The first variable is equity divided by total assets, which is a simple measure of capital adequacy. Banks with higher capital ratios are less likely to fail, so the coefficient on this variable should be negative. The second variable is construction loans divided by total assets and represents the extent to which the de novo bank specializes in this type of higher-risk commercial real estate lending. The coefficient sign of this variable should be positive, because more high-risk construction loans should increase the likelihood of failure.

Total nonperforming loans divided by total assets is used as an indicator of the quality or credit risk of the bank's loan portfolio.[19] More problem loans generally signal higher loan losses in the future and an increased risk of failure, so this variable should have a positive coefficient in the estimated equation. Pretax net operating income divided by total assets serves as a measure of overall profitability.[20] More profitable banks should be less likely to fail, implying a negative coefficient in the failure equation. The ratio of other noninterest expenses divided by total assets is also included as an independent variable. A wide variety of expenses fall into this category, including costs related to the resolution of problem assets.[21] Higher expenses imply an increased risk of failure and a positive coefficient sign in the failure equation. The average cost of interest-bearing deposits is included to capture the impact of differences in liability composition on the probability of failure. The coefficient on this variable should be positive, because de novo banks with higher liability costs, perhaps stemming from heavier reliance on brokered deposits, are more likely to fail.

---

[19] The numerator is the sum of total loans past due 30 to 89 days and still accruing, loans 90 or more days past due and still accruing, and nonaccrual loans.

[20] A pretax profitability variable is used in an attempt to control for differences in after-tax returns attributable to a sample bank's decision to adopt Subchapter S status.

[21] In addition to charges paid to others for repossession or collection of loans or assets, this category includes expenses related to data processing, advertising and marketing, directors' fees, printing, supplies, postage, legal fees, FDIC deposit insurance, accounting and auditing, consulting and advisory services, ATM and interchange fees, telecommunications, fees to state and/or federal supervisors, management fees to a parent holding company, litigation costs, and civil money penalties, as well as several other types of costs.

The value of each of these variables in a given time period is the average of the values in quarters t-4 and t-5. The first three ratios have end-of-quarter values in the numerators and denominators because they are constructed entirely from balance sheet data. Income statement data are used in the numerator of the last three ratios. In each of these measures, the annualized quarterly value of the respective numerator is divided by the end-of-quarter value of the denominator in t-4 and t-5 and then these two values are averaged.[22]

The last two of the eight bank-characteristic variables in the estimated equations are qualitative. One takes on a value of 1 for banks that were Subchapter S corporations in quarter t-4. The other variable is set equal to 1 if a bank had four or more offices in t-4.[23]

The expected effect of Subchapter S status on the likelihood of failure is unclear. There is some empirical evidence indicating that Subchapter S banks are more profitable than C corp banks even on a pretax basis.[24] If this is so, it implies a lower failure risk and a negative sign in the failure equation. But Subchapter S status might also result in higher risk as well. The primary reason for choosing the S corporation form is that it eliminates the double taxation of dividends. This creates an incentive for Subchapter S banks to increase the amount of dividends passed on to shareholders, who must pay any taxes on their pro-rata share of earnings. Higher dividends imply lower retained earnings over time, which in turn mean less internally generated equity capital. Subchapter S status also restricts a bank's freedom of action in several ways. Most notably, S corporations may have only a limited number of shareholders and issue one class of

---

[22] The values of the other noninterest expense and deposit cost variables are also Winsorized at the 1 and 99 percentile values.

[23] The cutoff is equal to the 75th percentile value for the sample banks.

[24] See, for example, Harvey and Padget (2000), p. 28, and Gilbert and Wheelock (2007), pp. 524-525.

stock.[25] Constraints on the number of shareholders may make it more difficult for S corporation banks to raise additional external capital if that becomes necessary.[26] Senior bank managers may also prefer to take on more risk because they typically have appreciable ownership stakes in the bank. If these effects are sufficiently powerful, Subchapter S status could increase the likelihood of failure.

The number of offices dummy is included to serve as a proxy for the extent of size-related cost savings and risk reduction stemming from greater geographic diversification. If it adequately represents the magnitudes of these benefits, it should have a negative coefficient in the failure equation.

The last three explanatory variables, selected from a long list of commonly used alternatives, are indicators of the nature of the local environment in which each sample bank operates. The first variable is the annual percentage change in per capita personal income in each bank's local economic market over the most recent previous year.[27] Demand for bank services should be higher in markets with higher income growth so the coefficient on this variable should be negative in the failure equation.

The second variable in this group is the average annual de novo entry rate in the relevant local market over the years t-2 and t-3.[28] This variable reflects entry by both de novo banks and

---

[25] The limit was set at 75 in 1996 and increased to 100 in 2004.

[26] This possibility is mentioned by Hodder, McAnally, and Weaver (2003).

[27] The local market for each de novo bank is defined as either the metropolitan or micropolitan statistical area or rural country where its headquarters office is located.

[28] For example, for a bank where the reference quarter represents 1997:Q3, the associated local market entry rate calculated using FDIC Summary of Deposit (SOD) data is the average of the annual entry rates for the periods June 1994–June 1995 and June 1995–June 1996.

out-of-market de novo branching activities by existing organizations.[29] The relationship between this variable and de novo failure is ambiguous. Lagged de novo entry could capture the effects of unobserved market attractiveness variables. If so, the variable would have a negative coefficient in a de novo failure equation. Alternatively, high de novo entry rates in the recent past mean more competition for new small banks operating in the market. This story implies higher lagged de novo entry will increase the likelihood of failure.

The third local market variable included in the failure equation is the average percentage of local market deposits acquired in nonconsolidation bank mergers over years t-2 and t-3.[30] The likely impact of the merger variable on de novo failure is also difficult to predict a priori. Available evidence indicates that entry is more likely in markets with more merger activity, especially when it involves expansion by large, out-of-market banking organizations absorbing smaller competitors. The explanation for this result is higher expected profitability for entrants stemming from a surfeit of small business and retail customers who prefer to deal with smaller local banks that offer high levels of personal service.

Greater levels of merger activity might also reflect market attractiveness. Both of these influences imply a lower failure risk. Conversely, new entrants might ultimately face stronger competition from surviving, more efficient entities after merger integration is completed. If so, the coefficient on the merger variable should be positive, indicating an increased risk of de novo bank failure.

---

[29] Adams and Amel (2007), p.11, argue in favor of this comprehensive entry measure.

[30] This means that the effects of intra-holding company consolidation mergers and holding company acquisitions are excluded. Because this variable is also constructed from SOD data, it is defined in the same way as the de novo entry measure described in the previous footnote.

The natural log of the number of quarters over which each bank was observed also appears on the right-hand side of the failure equation. The inclusion of this variable allows the baseline hazard rate to be time-dependent.[31] The coefficient on this variable should be positive, because it takes some time for any subsequent losses to exhaust de novo bank start-up capital.

A series of alternative supervisory choice variables was then added to the basic specification of the failure equation. First, a single initial supervisory choice dummy was added as an explanatory variable. This variable takes on a value of 1 in all time periods for de novo banks that initially chose a national charter and a zero otherwise. Thus, it does not reflect any subsequent changes in supervisor. The second alternative substitutes a supervisory choice dummy that takes on a value of 1 if a bank had the OCC as its supervisor in quarter t-1; otherwise it is set equal to zero. In the third specification, the initial OCC supervisory choice indicator is included along with a second dummy variable that captures any subsequent change in a bank's initial charter. This indicator is set equal to 1 for de novo banks that changed from a national to any state charter, or vice versa in every quarter after the shift. The fourth specification includes the same initial OCC supervisory dummy as version 3 but has a broader subsequent supervisory change dummy, which is set equal to 1 for all quarters after a bank made any type of primary federal supervisory change. This means that the supervisory change variable includes state-to-state flips. The fifth and last specification simply expands the supervisory change dummy to capture two different types of subsequent switches. One indicator takes on a value of 1 for banks that changed from an initial national to a state charter in a prior quarter. The other takes on a value of 1 for state-chartered banks that switched their primary federal supervisor in a prior quarter but did not become national banks.

---

[31] A number of different functions of time were tried in the estimated equation. The log transformation was simple and performed as well as or better than more complicated alternatives.

If a national charter imposes a sizeable, unavoidable cost burden on de novo banks, the coefficient on the initial OCC supervisory dummy should be positive, indicating greater risk relative to the state-chartered reference group used during estimation. The anticipated effects of the different types of subsequent supervisory change examined are less clear. For example, if switching from an initial national to a state charter after start-up reduces any supervisory cost disadvantage, de novo banks that do so should have a lower risk of failure. On the other hand, the current supervisor might push higher-risk banks to switch, or banks may be motivated to change their supervisor in hopes of facing looser constraints on their behavior. In both cases, banks that switch should be more likely to fail.

Because none of the banks that made state-to-national charter switches failed, it was not possible to estimate how this sort of change influenced the probability of de novo failure. A number of alternative estimation samples were created to determine if the results were sensitive to whether and how these banks were included in the analysis. To get baseline results all of the observations for the seven banks that made this change were included in the analysis. This approach means that these banks become part of the initially state-chartered reference group in all of the estimated equations, influencing the estimated coefficients on the supervisory choice and change variables that are included on the right-hand side. A second sample included observations for these banks only up to the quarter in which they switched their supervisor and charter and treated them as censored at that point. In a third sample all of the available observations for the seven banks were simply dropped. The latter two approaches imply that only one type of charter change will be observed, making it unnecessary to estimate the third version of the model described above. None of these adjustments in the estimation sample substantively altered any of the key results obtained using the complete sample. For this reason, and for the sake of brevity, the estimates obtained with the adjusted samples are not reported.

As noted at the end of section III.B, there were also four de novo banks that made two supervisory changes each over the observation period. Given the very small number of banks pursuing this strategy, no attempt was made to explicitly investigate the impact of a second switch. But adjustments in the estimation sample like the ones described in the paragraph above were made to determine if the results were sensitive to how these banks were treated in the analysis. First, all of the observations for these four banks are included and their second supervisory change is ignored. The basic equations were also re-estimated, treating these four banks as censored at the time of their second supervisory change. Finally, the basic equations were estimated after totally excluding the four banks from the sample. None of these adjustments dramatically altered the statistical results obtained using the complete sample and so are also not reported.

If de novo banks tend to merge because they cannot successfully compete as independent entities, the signs of the coefficients on the explanatory variables should generally be the same in both the merger and failure equations. For example, less profitable banks should be more likely to merge as well as fail. But it is also possible that some de novo banks sell out because the acquirers pay a premium to take control of well-run organizations with valuable franchises in attractive markets. In this case, merger likelihoods would increase with de novo profitability. Or the mixture of possible merger motives could result in an insignificant coefficient on profitability or other variables in the merger equation.

V.   The Results

Tables 5A, 5B, and 5C contain the results of estimating the five basic versions of the multinomial logit model using the largest possible number of sample observations. Because the relationship between supervisory choice and failure is the focus of this study, the estimated failure equations are examined first and most closely.

V.A.   The Estimated Failure Equations

The first version of the model reported in table 5A includes only a single initial national charter dummy implying OCC supervision on the right hand side of the estimated failure and merger equations. This specification explicitly ignores the large number and variety of subsequent supervisory changes by the sample banks that occurred after start-up. The estimated coefficient on the initial OCC supervisory dummy is positive in the failure equation but statistically insignificant.

In the second version of the model in table 5A, the initial national bank dummy is replaced by an alternative that reflects whether OCC supervision in quarter t-1 influenced the likelihood of failure in the subsequent quarter. This indicator won't reflect de novo banks that changed from an initial national to a state charter prior to t-1 but will incorporate those that made the opposite state-to-national conversion. The estimated coefficient on this variable is negative but statistically insignificant implying that there is no relationship between this supervisory choice measure and de novo failure.

Two supervisory choice variables appear in the equations in the third version of the estimated model reported in table 5B. The first is the same initial supervisory choice dummy used in version 1, which takes on a value of 1 for de novos that initially chose to be national banks. The second variable reflects a simultaneous change in charter and primary federal supervisor after start-up. This dummy variable is set equal to 1 for sample banks that changed their initial charter in quarter t-1 or earlier. Thus, this supervisory change indicator does not differentiate between national-to-state and state-to-national charter conversions. It also does not capture any subsequent state-to-state flips that involve a change in a state bank's primary federal supervisory without a charter change. When this specification is employed, the estimated coefficient on the initial OCC supervisory dummy is again positive but insignificant in the failure equation. The positive significant coefficient on the charter change variable indicates that failure risk is higher for de novo banks that subsequently changed their initial supervisor and charter.

In the fourth version of the model reported in table 5B, the same initial OCC dummy appears on the right hand side. The charter change dummy is replaced by a more broadly defined alternative that takes on a value of 1 for banks that made any change in their initial primary federal supervisor in quarter t-1 or earlier, including those that change their primary federal supervisor while retaining an initial state charter. This variable does not distinguish between alternative types of supervisory change and so the coefficient reflects the average effect of all possible changes. The results indicate that the initial choice of the OCC as primary supervisor has an insignificant impact on the likelihood of de novo failure. The estimated coefficient on this broader measure of supervisory change is positive and significant in the failure equation indicating de novo banks that change their initial supervisor in any way have a higher likelihood of failing.

In the fifth and final version of the model reported in table 5C, the single supervisory change variable used in version 5 is replaced with two separate dummy variables that capture different types of supervisory changes after start-up. One of these variables takes on a value of 1 for de novo banks that switched from an initial national charter to a state charter in or before quarter t-1. The other indicator is set equal to 1 for state banks that changed their primary federal supervisor in any way but not their charter in quarter t-1 or earlier. Once again, the initial national charter dummy is also included in the estimated equations.

The coefficient on the initial national charter and OCC supervision dummy is not significant in this last estimated version of the failure equation. This result means that de novo banks that make and never change this choice are not more likely to fail than the reference group of state banks. One possible explanation for the insignificant effect is that any explicit cost disadvantage related to a national charter is inconsequential or can be rendered so by an effective entry strategy. It also might reflect effects related to constraints on credit concentration and risk or slower growth due to tighter legal lending limits.

The supervisory change variables, however, do have significant positive coefficients in the last failure equation indicating that the switches increase the likelihood of de novo failure. The results reveal that de novos that exchanged their initial national charter for a state one and supervision by either the Federal Reserve or the FDIC, as well as state banks that changed their initial primary federal supervisor but not their charter are significantly more likely to fail. In fact, when dummies for both types of change are included in version 5 of the model, the values of the two coefficients are quite close, indicating that both types of change have similar impacts on the probability of de novo failure.[32]

There are a number of reasons de novo banks making one of the two types of supervisory change have higher failure probabilities, even when additional control variables are included in the estimated equation. Higher failure risk for de novos switching from national to state charters

---

[32] A formal test that they are equal does not result in a rejection of the hypothesis.

could reflect the effects of increased credit concentrations facilitated by higher legal lending limits.

This sort of shift, however, may also reflect the actions of an already troubled de novo bank shedding a charter-related cost disadvantage in an attempt to survive. It is possible that any sort of supervisory change relatively soon after start-up represents adverse information about unobserved management quality. Another explanation is that supervisory changes are a signal that a de novo bank is altering its strategy, which can increase risk.[33]

The coefficients on most of the explanatory variables in the failure equations conform to expectations based on previous empirical work. The results reveal that higher levels of construction lending by de novo banks significantly increase failure risk. The estimated coefficient on the nonperforming loan variable, an indicator of the level of problem assets at the bank, is also positive and significant in the failure equation. Conversely, the overall profitability measure has a negative significant coefficient, signaling that higher profitability is associated with a reduced likelihood of failure.

The results reveal that higher levels of other noninterest expenses significantly increase the probability of de novo failure. The estimated coefficient on the average cost of interest-bearing deposits is also positive and significant, supporting the reasonable notion that higher funding costs make failure more likely.

The coefficient on the Subchapter S indicator is positive and significant in every version of the failure equation estimated. This result is consistent with the notion that de novo banks organized in this way are riskier and more likely to fail.

---

[33] Empirical evidence in Whalen (2007) shows that changes in community bank lending strategy are associated with lower bank returns and higher risk.

The coefficient on the multiple office dummy is always positive and marginally significant in the failure equations. This effect does not support the notion that this variable is an indicator of greater geographic diversification. It could indicate that a larger office network imposes a relatively heavy overhead burden on new banks raising their likelihood of failure.

In all of the failure equations, the estimated coefficient on the local market per capita personal income growth variable is negative and significant, as expected. The results show that higher past bank entry rates in the local market significantly increase the probability of de novo failure. This finding may reflect more intense competition by these new bank entrants. The estimated coefficient on the merger variable is consistently negative and significant in the failure equations. This relationship is consistent with the notion that higher merger activity increases the pool of profitable potential customers for de novo banks or reflects unobserved measures of market attractiveness.

The coefficient on the log time variable also is positive and significant in all of the estimated failure equations. This result suggests that the risk of de novo failure is positively but nonlinearly related to time after start-up.

V.B.   The Estimated Merger Equations

The estimated effects of the supervisory choice and change variables on the likelihood that a de novo bank disappears through merger differ from the pattern exhibited in the related failure equations. In all of the merger equations where the initial OCC supervisory choice dummy is included, the estimated coefficient is positive and significant, indicating that de novo national banks are more likely to disappear through merger than state-chartered bank peers. Modest actual or perceived charter-related disadvantages are one possible explanation for this relationship. Another is that this supervisory choice variable reflects the impacts of correlated unobserved factors that influence merger likelihoods.[34]

All of the subsequent supervisory change variables turn out to be insignificant in every version of the merger equations estimated. Apparently, de novo bank acquirers do not expect supervisory changes to fundamentally or permanently alter the performance of potential targets.

The revealed effects of the other control variables generally suggest that less profitable, riskier de novo banks that do not fail are also more likely to disappear through merger. As in the related failure equations, the estimated coefficients show that increases in construction lending, higher other operating expenses, and lower profitability significantly increase the probability of a de novo bank merger.

The only other bank characteristic variable that has a significant impact in the merger equations is the Subchapter S dummy. The results indicate that Subchapter S banks are significantly less likely to disappear through merger, the opposite of the influence evident in the failure equation. This effect has been found in previous research.[35] A likely explanation is that current shareholders earn or expect to earn higher after-tax returns from Subchapter S banks and so are less inclined to sell.

---

[34] One candidate is multibank holding company (MBHC) affiliation. Unlike non-MBHC banks, MBHC affiliates can merge into either an unaffiliated or affiliated bank if the parent consolidates previously owned subsidiaries. When an MBHC affiliation variable is added to the right-hand side of a logit model explaining de novo merger probability, its coefficient is positive and highly significant, while the initial OCC choice dummy becomes insignificant. The MBHC variable is not included in the multinomial logit models because preliminary analysis revealed that it was not a significant determinant of de novo failure.

[35] See Mehran and Suher (2009).

VI. Summary and Conclusions

This study examines the impact of the initial and subsequent supervisory choices of de novo banks on the likelihood that they either failed or merged. The data show that more than 7 percent of the 1,015 de novo banks that began operations during the interval from 1996:Q3 through 2003:Q1 changed their initial primary federal supervisors by the end of 2010:Q2. More than half of these supervisory changes also involved charter conversions, with shifts away from the OCC to either the Federal Reserve or the FDIC accounting for more than 80 percent of the charter changes.

The empirical analysis indicates that de novo banks that did not revisit their initial decision to operate with a national charter and OCC supervision are not more likely to fail than the state bank reference group. Therefore, while the net shift away from OCC supervision is consistent with a perceived disadvantage, apparently having national charters does not entail an insurmountable actual performance handicap for de novo banks. The fact that some state banks switched to national charters and none subsequently failed reinforces this conclusion.

The evidence does show that some, but not all, types of subsequent supervisory changes are associated with a higher probability of de novo failure. Specifically, the results of the estimated competing risk models reveal that de novo banks exchanging initial national charters for state charters and supervision by either the Federal Reserve or FDIC, as well as state banks that changed their initial primary federal supervisor but not their charter are significantly more likely to fail. Although data issues preclude a more rigorous model-based investigation, less sophisticated analysis revealed that none of the state banks that shifted to national charters and OCC supervision after start-up failed.

The estimated equations show that the measures of supervisory choice have different effects on the probability of de novo merger. De novo banks initially choosing national charters have a significantly higher likelihood of being merged, all else being equal. Neither of the supervisory change variables have a significant influence on merger probabilities in any of the versions of the estimated model.

The results clearly show that supervisory changes post-start-up have an important influence on de novo bank survival, and should not be ignored in analyses of other aspects of their performance. Additional research on this topic is warranted to see if similar findings are evident for more mature banks and different time periods. Investigation of the sensitivity of these findings to variations in the time lag between supervisory changes and failure or other performance metrics also would be informative.

VII. References

Adams, R., and D. Amel. 2007. "The Effects of Past Entry, Market Consolidation, and Expansion by Incumbents on the Probability of Entry." Board of Governors of the Federal Reserve System Finance and Economics Discussion Series. Working Paper 2007–51.

Gilbert, R.A., and D. Wheelock. 2007. "Measuring Commercial Bank Profitability: Proceed With Caution." Federal Reserve Bank of St. Louis *Review*. November/December.

Harvey, J., and J. Padget. 2000. "Subchapter S—A New Tool for Enhancing the Value of Community Banks." *Financial Industry Perspectives*. Kansas City, Mo: Federal Reserve Bank of Kansas City.

Hodder, L., M. McAnally, and C. Weaver. 2003. "The Influence of Tax and Nontax Factors on Banks' Choice of Organizational Form." *The Accounting Review* 78, 1: 297–25.

Mehran, H., and M. Suher. 2009. "The Impact of Tax Law Changes on Bank Dividend Policy, Sell-Offs, Organizational Form, and Industry Structure." Federal Reserve Bank of New York Staff Report No. 369.

Rosen, R. 2005. "Switching Primary Federal Regulators: Is It Beneficial for U.S. Banks?" Federal Reserve Bank of Chicago *Economic Perspectives*. Issue 3Q.

Whalen, G. 2007. "Community Bank Strategic Lending Choices and Performance." OCC Economics Working Paper 2007-3. Washington: Office of the Comptroller of the Currency. July.

Whalen, G. 2010. "Early Life Performance Differences Between De Novo National and State Banks." Draft.

Wheelock, D., and P. Wilson. 2000. "Why Do Banks Disappear? The Determinants of U.S. Bank Failures and Acquisitions." *Review of Economics and Statistics*. 82 No. 1.

Table 1: Quarterly Bank Failure Data, First Quarter 2008 Through Fourth Quarter 2010

Quarter	Number of commercial bank failures	OCC-supervised	Percent of all failures	Federal Reserve-supervised	Percent of all failures	FDIC-supervised	Percent of all failures	Bank less than 10 years old at failure	Percent of all failures
2008									
1st	2	1	50.0	0	0.0	1	50.0	0	0.0
2nd	2	2	100.0	0	0.0	0	0.0	0	0.0
3rd	6	2	33.3	0	0.0	4	66.7	3	50.0
4th	9	0	0.0	1	11.1	8	88.9	4	44.4
2009									
1st	20	5	25.0	2	10.0	13	65.0	6	30.0
2nd	21	3	14.3	3	14.3	15	71.4	9	42.9
3rd	42	5	11.9	5	11.9	32	76.2	10	23.8
4th	37	12	32.4	6	16.2	19	51.4	9	24.3
2010									
1st	35	5	14.3	5	14.3	25	71.4	8	22.9
2nd	39	7	17.9	2	5.1	30	76.9	12	30.8
3rd	31	6	19.4	6	19.4	19	61.3	7	22.6
4th	27	5	18.5	4	14.8	18	66.7	6	22.2
Total	271	53	19.6	34	12.5	184	67.9	74	27.3

Table 2: Number and Percent of De Novo Banks by Initial Federal Supervisor, 1993–2009, by De Novo Bank Start Year

	1993	1994	1995	1996	1997	1998	1999	2000	2001	2002	2003	2004	2005	2006	2007	2008	2009	Total
(1) De novo national banks	5	15	18	41	43	46	51	38	31	29	11	17	19	20	24	8	7	423
(2) Percent of column total	14.3	35.7	20.7	32.0	25.3	26.3	22.9	21.1	25.8	33.0	10.6	14.8	11.9	11.4	14.8	9.3	31.8	20.4
(3) De novo state member Banks	4	3	11	6	12	17	30	12	14	2	6	7	7	17	11	8	0	167
(4) Percent of column total	11.4	7.1	12.6	4.7	7.1	9.7	13.5	6.7	11.7	2.3	5.8	6.1	4.4	9.7	6.8	9.3	0.0	8.1
(5) De novo state nonmember banks	26	24	58	81	115	112	142	130	75	57	87	91	134	139	127	70	15	1,483
(6) Percent of column total	74.3	57.1	66.7	63.3	67.6	64.0	63.7	72.2	62.5	64.8	83.7	79.1	83.8	79.0	78.4	81.4	68.2	71.5
(7) Total de novo state banks	30	27	69	87	127	129	172	142	89	59	93	98	141	156	138	78	15	1,650
(8) Percent of column total	85.7	64.3	79.3	68.0	74.7	73.7	77.1	78.9	74.2	67.0	89.4	85.2	88.1	88.6	85.2	90.7	68.2	79.6
(9) Total de novo banks	35	42	87	128	170	175	223	180	120	88	104	115	160	176	162	86	22	2,073

Table 3: Outcomes for De Novo Banks With Initial National Charters Beginning Operations From Third Quarter 1996 Through First Quarter 2003

	Sample totals	No change in primary federal supervisor from start date through 6/30/2010	Changed initial primary federal supervisor by 6/30/2010
Total number	249	217	32
Number failing by 6/30/2010	13	8	5
Number voluntarily merging by 6/30/2010	101	94	7
Number surviving through 6/30/2010	135	115	20

Table 4: Outcomes for De Novo Banks With Initial State Charters Beginning Operations From Third Quarter 1996 Through First Quarter 2003

	Sample totals	No change in initial primary federal supervisor through 6/30/2010	Changed initial primary federal supervisor to OCC by 6/30/2010	Changed initial primary federal supervisor to FRB/FDIC by 6/30/2010	Changed initial primary federal supervisor by 6/30/2010
Total number	766	723	7	36	43
Number failing by 6/30/2010	46	42	0	4	4
Number voluntarily merging by 6/30/2010	255	237	4	14	18
Number surviving through 6/30/2010	465	444	3	18	21

Table 5A: Competing Risk Models, Multinomial Logit Discrete Time Hazard Model of De Novo Bank Failure Versus Voluntary Merger, Complete Sample

Explanatory variables	Version 1				Version 2			
	Merger equation		Failure equation		Merger equation		Failure equation	
	Coef	z	Coef	z	Coef	z	Coef	z
Initial de novo national charter	0.2791	2.28	0.4952	1.24				
National charter t-1					0.3131	2.53	-0.0330	-0.07
Bank changed charter in a prior quarter								
Bank changed primary federal supervisor in a prior quarter								
Bank switched from initial national to state charter in a prior quarter								
Bank kept initial state charter but changed primary federal supervisor in a prior quarter								
Average equity/total assets	0.0019	0.16	-0.5723	-3.57	0.0020	0.16	-0.5816	-3.62
Average construction loans/total assets	0.0125	2.37	0.0605	4.17	0.0129	2.44	0.0604	4.22
Average total nonperforming loans/total assets	0.0280	0.92	0.1841	5.32	0.0294	0.97	0.1747	5.37
Average pretax net income/total assets	-0.0413	-2.31	-0.1217	-4.24	-0.0401	-2.25	-0.1221	-4.34
Average other noninterest expenses/total assets	0.1925	1.82	0.5909	2.12	0.1879	1.77	0.6363	2.30
Average total deposit interest expense/total interest-bearing deposits	-0.0641	-1.25	0.5562	3.16	-0.0639	-1.25	0.5472	3.11
Multiple office dummy	0.0300	0.21	0.6866	1.94	0.0277	0.20	0.7503	2.12
Subchapter S Corp Form	-0.8448	-3.52	0.7779	2.26	-0.8465	-3.53	0.7968	2.40
Market per capita personal income growth	0.0086	0.42	-0.1907	-2.56	0.0089	0.44	-0.1992	-2.66
Average local market entry rate	0.0112	1.01	0.0544	2.11	0.0109	0.98	0.0534	2.17
Average percentage of market deposits acquired in bank mergers	0.0031	0.25	-0.2102	-2.78	0.0030	0.24	-0.2160	-2.89
Log time	0.4909	5.13	1.1374	3.43	0.4916	5.15	1.1482	3.59
Constant	-6.1573	-16.36	-9.2587	-5.16	-6.1658	-16.49	-9.0533	-5.12
Wald chi2	507.65				515.72			
Pseudo R2	0.1065				0.1064			
Number of observations	31,899				31,899			
Number of sample banks	1,015				1,015			

Table 5B: Competing Risk Models, Multinomial Logit Discrete Time Hazard Model of De Novo Bank Failure Versus Voluntary Merger, Complete Sample

Explanatory variables	Version 3 Merger equation Coef	z	Version 3 Failure equation Coef	z	Version 4 Merger equation Coef	z	Version 4 Failure equation Coef	z
Initial de novo national charter	0.2729	2.18	0.1416	0.31	0.2711	2.21	0.2669	0.67
National charter t-1								
Bank changed charter in a prior quarter	0.0862	0.28	1.6167	2.82	0.2426	1.16	1.6097	3.84
Bank changed primary federal supervisor in a prior quarter								
Bank switched from initial national to state charter in a prior quarter								
Bank kept initial state charter but changed primary federal supervisor in a prior quarter								
Average equity/total assets	0.0017	0.13	-0.5918	-3.73	0.0010	0.08	-0.5977	-3.70
Average construction loans/total assets	0.0125	2.35	0.0588	3.90	0.0121	2.28	0.0591	3.74
Average total nonperforming loans/total assets	0.0281	0.92	0.1888	5.37	0.0293	0.96	0.1971	5.35
Average pretax net income/total assets	-0.0410	-2.29	-0.1179	-4.16	-0.0410	-2.31	-0.1181	-4.13
Average other noninterest expenses/total assets	0.1929	1.82	0.5801	2.09	0.1925	1.82	0.5843	2.08
Average total deposit interest expense/total interest-bearing deposits	-0.0645	-1.25	0.4964	2.81	-0.0645	-1.26	0.4825	2.77
Multiple office dummy	0.0285	0.20	0.7033	1.96	0.0216	0.15	0.7266	2.04
Subchapter S Corp Form	-0.8456	-3.52	0.7930	2.38	-0.8444	-3.52	0.8366	2.48
Market per capita personal income growth	0.0084	0.41	-0.1843	-2.44	0.0084	0.42	-0.1938	-2.56
Average local market entry rate	0.0113	1.02	0.0591	2.27	0.0114	1.03	0.0584	2.21
Average percentage of market deposits acquired in bank mergers	0.0030	0.24	-0.2171	-2.83	0.0027	0.21	-0.2208	-2.88
Log time	0.4887	5.09	1.1238	3.29	0.4805	5.00	1.0310	3.16
Constant	-6.1469	-16.23	-8.8535	-5.07	-6.1234	-16.23	-8.6034	-4.89
Wald chi2	508.62				510.27			
Pseudo R2	0.1076				0.1089			
Number of observations	31,899				31,899			
Number of sample banks	1,015				1,015			

Table 5C: Competing Risk Models, Multinomial Logit Discrete Time Hazard Model of De Novo Bank Failure Versus Voluntary Merger, Complete Sample

Explanatory variables	Version 5			
	Merger equation		Failure equation	
	Coef	z	Coef	z
Initial de novo national charter	0.3090	2.44	0.2085	0.42
National charter t-1				
Bank changed charter in a prior quarter				
Bank changed primary federal supervisor in a prior quarter				
Bank switched from initial national to state charter in a prior quarter	−0.1576	−0.41	1.7372	2.77
Bank kept initial state charter but changed primary federal supervisor in a prior quarter	0.3653	1.32	1.5617	2.75
Average equity/total assets	0.0020	0.16	−0.5993	−3.70
Average construction loans/total assets	0.0124	2.34	0.0590	3.73
Average total nonperforming loans/total assets	0.0297	0.97	0.1966	5.33
Average pretax net income/total assets	−0.0418	−2.36	−0.1178	−4.11
Average other noninterest expenses/total assets	0.1894	1.78	0.5842	2.08
Average total deposit interest expense/total interest-bearing deposits	−0.0622	−1.21	0.4733	2.71
Multiple office dummy	0.0255	0.18	0.7331	2.05
Subchapter S Corp Form	−0.8404	−3.50	0.8326	2.46
Market per capita personal income growth	0.0091	0.44	−0.1923	−2.56
Average local market entry rate	0.0108	0.98	0.0587	2.22
Average percentage of market deposits acquired in bank mergers	0.0026	0.21	−0.2202	−2.85
Log time	0.4871	5.09	1.0293	3.12
Constant	−6.1664	−16.33	−8.5395	−4.83
Wald chi2	510.48			
Pseudo R2	0.1091			
Number of observations	31,899			
Number of sample banks	1,015